PRAISE FOR *A VIEW FROM ACROSS THE NET*

"Curly Davis is an inspirational tennis instructor and a motivational mentor. He consistently shares his 'Curly-isms' and life lessons with his loyal clients and his professional teaching skills. This book is a testament to a life well lived, full of lessons on and off the tennis court. Humorous, poignant, and entertaining—not just for tennis enthusiasts—I highly recommend this book to all who live life as a work in progress."

—Dr. Paul Rogers
Vice-Chair of the Board of Visitors
College of Science and Liberal Arts, New Jersey Institute of Technology

"This book is about so much more than tennis. Curly Davis is a master storyteller who happens to be a tennis coach. His tales bring to life the many lessons he has learned from decades of helping people, both on and off the tennis court. Curly is funny, wise, observant, and passionate about what he loves: people and the crazy world we live in. Be prepared to laugh, cry, and be entertained by one of the best—if not THE best—storyteller."

—Craig Wood
CEO, Premier International

"I have dabbled with tennis throughout my life and never took a lesson until I met Curly Davis. Immediately, I was struck by his special way of communicating tennis instructions which were rich with life lessons. He was not just teaching tennis, he was modeling successful behavior patterns. He does this by sharing his experiences via his innate storytelling skills—which are often funny, inspiring, or enlightening—while subliminally supporting his masterful tennis teachings. Combine those traits with his global tennis and life experiences, and you have a best-in-class tennis *and* life coach. This book is inevitably filled with all his wonderful, witty wisdom.

"P.S. Never wear a golf shirt to a tennis lesson!"

—David Doubek
President, Medication Management Partners

"Wow, Curly is truly an amazing teacher of tennis, a savant of life experiences, and an incredible individual of the highest character. He blends his passion for the game of tennis with an infusion of humor combined with an awesome ability to share stories to help illustrate his point. My only regret is not knowing him for a longer period of time, as I would love to utilize his amazing life experiences beyond the tennis court to make myself a better person. He is a jewel of a man."

—Jim Erben
CEO, Erben & Associates

"A View From Across the Net is a gift for teachers and storytellers everywhere. Curly Davis inspires his students and readers to not only *do* better but *be* better. His skillful use of humor, braised in southern charm, will have your laughing out loud. But similar to a perfectly constructed tennis point, there are surprises along the way that will keep you on your toes. Davis's finely honed observational skills are used to great effect to craft memorable stories that motivate and inspire. Well done, Coach!

—Patrick Falso
President, Allegro Design Inc.

A View From Across the Net

A View From Across the Net

Life Lessons from My Fifty Years as a Tennis Pro

Curly Davis

The author has tried to recreate events, locations, and conversations from his/her memories of them. The author has made every effort to give credit to the source of any images, quotes, or other material contained within and obtain permissions when feasible.

Copyright © 2023 by Curly Davis

All rights reserved. No part of this book may be reproduced or transmitted in any form or by any means, electronic or mechanical, including photocopying, recording, or any information storage and retrieval system, without permission in writing from the author.

ISBN: 978-1-6653-0375-0 - Paperback
eISBN: 978-1-6653-0376-7 - ePub

This ISBN is the property of BookLogix for the express purpose of sales and distribution of this title. BookLogix is not responsible for the writing or design/appearance of this book. The content of this book is the property of the copyright holder only. BookLogix does not hold any ownership of the content of this book and is not liable in any way for the materials contained within. The views and opinions expressed in this book are the property of the Author/Copyright holder, and do not necessarily reflect those of BookLogix.

0 6 0 7 2 3

∞This paper meets the requirements of ANSI/NISO Z39.48-1992 (Permanence of Paper)

I dedicate this book to all the tennis players who honored me with the opportunity to teach them the game of tennis and sometimes pass along a few "life lessons."

This dedication is seriously one from the heart, both figuratively and literally.

To my wife, Mikki, whose love inspires and sustains me as I strive to be the best version of myself in all areas of my life.

Contents

Foreword ix

Preface xv

Chapter One 1

Gallery 59

Chapter Two 65

Foreword

In 2015, I played in a tennis tournament in Naples, Florida. I was in the finals against an excellent player, and I knew it would be a hard-fought match. I was playing well and won the first set 6–4. When I was up 5–2 in the second set, I noticed a pressure in my chest that radiated to my left armpit. I remembered a conversation with my father, who has since passed, about his chest pains; he had described the same symptoms to me—chest pressure and a left-armpit itching.

As my opponent drew closer in the score, I got my thoughts back on tennis. I pulled out the second set 6–4 and won the match.

On Sunday, the next day, I taught Dr. Rick Beatty, an eye doctor client/friend, and told him of my symptoms. He dropped his racket and immediately went to his phone. I stopped him from calling anyone, and he acquiesced only after I agreed to allow him to set up a doctor's appointment for me.

I went to the appointment he arranged the following day, but the receptionist informed me that the doctor did not accept my insurance. When I told Rick about the insurance issue, he set me up with another doctor, Dr. Richard Prewitt, another tennis player, for Wednesday of that week.

At Dr. Prewitt's, I informed them of the pressure in my chest that radiated to my left armpit. They immediately placed me in a wheelchair and wheeled me to the emergency room. The attending doctor was the one I had been scheduled to see on Monday.

He said, "I was supposed to see you on Monday. What happened?" I told him about the insurance issue, and he responded, "Well, now I have to see you since you came to the emergency room." He ran some tests before coming back and telling me, "You have some blocked heart arteries, and we need to keep you to perform an angioplasty."

I told him I would prefer to do that the following Monday (remember, this was Wednesday), so I had time to tell my clients I was to take a vacation, and I'd be back in a week.

The doctor said, "You won't be back on Monday."

I responded, "I promise I'll come back in."

The doctor then said something that got my attention about how serious this heart issue was: "No, you don't understand. You have what we call 'the widow maker'—a heart condition where you feel okay, then you die suddenly. So, you won't be back in on Monday, because you'll be dead."

I stayed in the hospital and had the angioplasty the following day. I went into surgery anesthetized, but when I came out of it, they informed me that my arteries were too clogged for the angioplasty. I needed a heart bypass, and heart-bypass surgery was not performed at this hospital.

Unfortunately, the doctor told me that the hospital I needed to go to had no beds available until the following week. So, they sent me home with strict instructions not to do *anything*—no tennis, no teaching, no leaving my house—just sit and do nothing.

I have a remarkably close friend, Deb Chartier, who heard about my heart situation and started looking after me. She did errands for me, helped me get a living will, and prepared and witnessed a last will.

I met with the heart doctor at the surgical hospital on Tuesday to discuss my alternatives. He analyzed my X-rays and the reports from the previous doctor. He told me I had three arteries that were 60 percent closed and needed bypass surgery, but the hospital didn't take my insurance. The only way around this was to go to the emergency room on Thursday and inform the ER people that he was my heart doctor. Meanwhile, he reserved the surgery room for that Friday.

My friend drove me to the ER and ran inside to inform them I was having heart issues; they immediately took me in and called the doctor. The following morning, I was going to receive a three-bypass surgery. My friend then called my brother. He and his wife came to the hospital, and I was able to see them before I went in for surgery.

On Saturday, the day after surgery, I came out of the fog and heard the doctor over my bed, talking to my brother, sister-in-law, and Deb. The doctor told them I had a five-bypass surgery. I spoke up and said, "No, just three." After opening me up, the doctor informed me that they saw I needed five arteries done, thus the five-bypass procedure.

On Monday, I was released from the hospital to go home for a month of recovery and doing nothing. (But, looking on the "bright side," Wimbledon was on during some of my recovery, so I had something to watch.)

Now, the miracle part of the story starts. My friend Deb had scheduled players from the entire Naples tennis community to come to my condominium to be with me and make sure all was okay. I didn't know many of these tennis players; what brought us together was tennis and, more importantly, their generous hearts. So, for one week, I had revolving "caregivers," all arranged by Deb. Per the doctor's request, Deb stayed with me for seven days, spending the night in the other bedroom listening to the baby monitor in my room, ready for any potential issues that may occur during the night.

These "caregivers" brought me food, offered to do laundry, or simply sat and read while I napped.

After that first week, I was at home alone, still recovering, when I had a phone call from three friends—Denmark Rushing and Mary and Paul Benzing. They asked if they could come over. I said, "Sure." They wanted to talk about my finances. They were aware that I was an independent contractor, receiving no salary or benefits, and wanted to help financially. I appreciated their offer and received it in the manner given, both loving and caring. I informed them that I had saved money for a rainy day and could get by, although I was aware I would be paying the hospital and surgery bills for the rest of my life.

Another two tennis friends, Rhonda and Neil, offered to organize a party for my benefit. They would auction off rackets, a high-end automobile for the weekend, and other items, all donated by friends of mine or the tennis community of Naples. The date arrived, and when I walked into the party, I was quite moved by the size of the crowd—even my brother and sister-in-law had made a surprise visit for the party!

After going around and personally thanking everyone for being there, I said a few words. I remember only some of what I said, but this in particular: "We are all here because of my heart, but you're here showing me your heart, and I thank you." I was incredibly moved and thanked Rhonda and Neil for organizing the event, the Naples tennis community, and my brother and his wife for their support. Afterward, I got in my car and sat and cried, appreciating what God and the people of Naples had done for me. But it wasn't over yet.

Paul Benzing gave me the name of a woman, a former hospital administrator, who he said might be able to help get my hospital bills reduced. I met with her, setting up an appointment with the hospital collection division. It was a short meeting where we gave the hospital collection person all the information. They told us that any decision would take fourteen days and that we should check back then. I called two weeks later and asked the hospital administrator for the status of my case.

She said, "It was sent to charity."

I asked, "What does that mean?"

She said, "You owe nothing."

I was absolutely floored!

I asked, "What about the doctor's bill and the X-rays?"

She said, "You'll have to check with them."

I did, and I received the same response "It's been sent to charity." I sat at my desk at home and cried, thanked God, and prayed for the tennis community.

Finally, I received a bill for $5,500 from another hospital where I had spent one night. That same afternoon, Rhonda and Neil called and asked to come over. I said, "Sure." They arrived and gave me the money they had collected at the party. It came to $5,100—almost exactly the amount I owed! Another miracle!

As you read this story, you can see why I dedicate this book to tennis players—both those I know and those I have yet to meet. The players I have taught have helped me become a better person and a better coach along the way. They provided many of the stories you are about to read.

Finally, I have to recognize a person who has been quietly supportive throughout all my heart procedure, afterward and to today—a great person and friend, Richard Fresne, a true angel to me and others.

Thank you all for all you have done for me, a thank-you from the "Repaired Heart."

Preface

In my fifty-plus years of teaching tennis, I have learned a great deal of what you will read from fellow tennis-teaching professionals or other sports figures, which I have labeled "community knowledge," discovered by listening and reading.

A little background: When asked at fourteen years old, "what do you want to be when you grow up?" my reply was, "a tennis-teaching professional." Even then, I never wanted to be an "ordinary" tennis pro; I wanted to be the best! I started being a "student of the game" by keeping a binder of tennis articles I clipped out of *World Tennis Magazine*, which is no longer published.

For a time in my coaching career, I taught only juniors of all levels. To get to know each student, I would ask them, "If you could have money or fame, which would you choose?" I received many excellent answers. To answer my own question was easy; I was not interested then nor now in the money. Do not get me wrong, I like money and what it offers. But what motivates me to get up and do what I do with enthusiasm every day is running away from being an ordinary tennis pro.

> *Normality is a paved road. It's comfortable to walk, but no flowers grow on it.*
> —Vincent van Gogh

> *As an artist signs their painting for the world to know, my students are my signature.*
> —Curly Davis

I am not trying to be typical but to be the best for the client in front of me, and if I do that, I have fulfilled my goal for that day.

I was not always of that thinking. Candidly, I remember some time ago, back in my twenties, I resented being labeled a "teacher" because I didn't want to be a teacher, like a schoolteacher. That changed in 1981. I have changed my thoughts and way of looking at the teaching profession.

You see, up until that time, I was a lousy tennis-teaching pro; I was selfish, late to lessons, or didn't show up for appointments, and, frankly, didn't care. What happened was, I took a hard look at my life and saw that drinking alcohol was the ruler in my life. You see, all my dreams of teaching tennis were fading away due to my drinking. Drinking alcohol is an elevator ride; it's either going up or down, and for me, it was going to the basement.

On March 29, 1981, I got off the elevator ride going down, and now it's on the way back up. It all started by putting down the bottle, picking up the phone, and asking for help. When I asked for help, I received hope—hope in a better life, hope in a better me. From hope grew faith, and I am not just talking about a spiritual belief but faith in others to teach me how to live life sober one day at a time because I sure did not know how to do that. I also received faith in myself to live life *doing the next right thing*. I received faith in God to "lead me where He needs me"; in short, His will for me daily.

From the elevator ride going up, many honors went from the Hall of *Shame* to the Kentucky Hall of *Fame*. I proudly inform you that I was inducted into the Kentucky Tennis Hall of Fame. Finally, and most importantly, I received love—the greatest love of all: the love of oneself.

I tell you the aforementioned because I have looked for God's will for me every day and His wisdom to guide me on what to say and teach. A lot of what I've learned I apply to my tennis teaching.

CHAPTER ONE

STORIES THAT WILL INSPIRE, INSTRUCT, OR MAKE YOU LAUGH

THE HAT VS. THE COMB

As a junior tennis player, we had many friends and we all played in local tournaments, so we knew each other's tennis games and abilities quite well. Two such friends of mine, Bob Lovett and Theodore Robertson. Bob is a crafty right-handed tennis player, two-handed strokes on both sides. Bob's one character flaw or strength depends on how you look at it: he was a little unpredictable on and off the court, weird, some would say. Theodore was a tall, skinny, very conservative, Catholic—the opposite of Bob.

Bob and Theodore had played many times before, and Bob easily won every time, with not much competition from Theodore; Bob always won 6–1 or 6–2. On one occasion, Theodore was playing against Bob, and Theodore showed up wearing a wildly colored shorts, shirt, and hat, none of which matched; the color combination was quite distracting. Remember, Theodore was very conservative; this tennis outfit was totally out of character, and it bothered Bob. Bob was so disturbed by the "outfit" that he started to lose, which had never happened before when they played! Bob began to yell at Theodore to "take off that silly-looking hat!" Theodore was not about to; he was winning! A crowd of us juniors started to gather because of the yelling. Bob was losing to Theodore, which had never happened before. Throughout the first set, Bob yelled, "Take off that hat!" But Theodore never did, and Theodore won the first set 6–4.

Before the second set started, Bob, quite frustrated, went over to his tennis racket cover. (Back then, we didn't have any tennis bags, so we carried all of our items—wallet, car keys, etc.—in a tennis racket cover.) He started to look inside, and Bob pulled out a comb, looked at Theodore, and said, "You're going to take the hat off your head."

Theodore replied, "No!"

Bob proceeded to place the comb in his mouth and play the second set like that! What a sight! Now Theodore was frustrated and distracted by Bob and the comb in his mouth. After every point, whoever lost the point ordered the other.

"Take that comb out of your mouth!" The response was, "Not until you take the silly hat off your head." Back and forth: "Take the hat off," "Take the comb out of your mouth."

The second set was close, with Bob winning it 7–5.

The third set started, comb in mouth and hat on head. The first point of the third set, Theodore served the ball, worked his way to the net; Bob gave him a weak lob that Theodore proceeded to dump in the bottom of the net! Theodore took the hat off his head and threw it to the side of the court; Bob took the comb out of his mouth and threw it to the side of the court. Result: Bob beat Theodore like he always did—6–1!

"Ignore the noise; focus on your work."

—Unknown

Remembering Names

As a tennis instructor, we meet many tennis players and cannot remember everyone's name. I heard if you related the name to something or someone famous, you have a better chance of remembering their name.

On this occurrence, I was having trouble remembering Patsy, my first lesson of the day on a Monday. I started thinking about how I could remember her name and thought, *Patsy—Patsy Cline, a country singer. GREAT! I got it.*

The following Monday arrived, I was on the court with Patsy, and once again, I had trouble remembering her name. Still, I had a plan: "country singer." Out of my mouth with such confidence, I said, "So Loretta, how you are hitting the tennis ball?" Luckily, she did not hear me, and I quickly recovered and remembered her name.

"If you can't remember my name, just say 'donuts,' and I'll turn around and look."

—Unknown

Word Fusing

We have all had this happen to us, where we fuse two words and out comes another word. During a lesson with Clara, a sweet, churchgoing, petite, attractive novice lady who had never played tennis before, that happened to me. She was a quick learner and moved quite quickly in her learning in the first lesson. My attempt to compliment her on her rapid learning skills was where I got in trouble. I tried to tell her she had been learning so quickly, she was on her second lesson plan or her next lesson. Well, I fused second and next together and out came, "you are learning so quickly you are actually on your sex lesson."

She jokingly responded, "I heard about you tennis pros."

"A good laugh and a long sleep are the best cures for anything."
—Irish Proverb

Words That Sound Alike and Could Get You in Trouble

When I worked with juniors, I offered a "morning madness" to the juniors. This was a five to six a.m. clinic on Mondays, Wednesdays, and Fridays, before they went to school. On one such session, a senior in high school, Anna, with a southern accent, arrived to play, but she forgot to do some homework the night before. She was sitting on the bleachers right next to the courts, doing homework and looking up on occasion. She looked up at one point and saw Harry, a freshman in high school, running around and over a bunch of tennis balls on the court to get to a ball. She was trying to warn him to watch out, that he was running through an obstacle course, but what came out was funny: "Watch out, honey, you're running through an intercourse." We all laughed and the next session, someone placed up a sign, reading, "watch out . . . intercourse crossing."

"Promise yourself . . . to be too large for worry, too noble for anger, too strong for fear, and too happy to permit the presence of trouble."
—Christian D. Larson

Best Lesson I Was Given on Teaching Tennis

I was a nineteen-year-old tennis pro/manager in Lexington, Kentucky. My dad and mom were driving down from Louisville, Kentucky, to spend the day with me but not until after I gave a lesson. I was giving the lesson to a beginner, and halfway through, my father came and sat down next to the tennis court to watch and listen. As all sons want their father's approval, I was no different. I greeted my dad and introduced him to the client. After the formalities, the client and I went back to the court, where I started to instruct some more. The lesson came to an end, the client left, and my dad placed his arm around me and gave me a great lesson on teaching: *"Son, what you said was good . . . but you said too much."* I will never forget that simple lesson to this day, and it's served me well.

"The best advice I could give anyone is to spend your time working on whatever you are passionate about in life."
—Richard Branson

Are You a Wandering and Wondering Generality?

In doubles, I often observe players while the point is still in play, wandering around aimlessly, hoping they will be in the right place at the right time. This is what I refer to as a "wandering and wondering generality."

To the novice eye, the tennis ball caroming around the court looks much like a random ball in a pinball machine, but to the trained eye, we know every shot should serve a purpose.

One story of mine demonstrates this "wandering and wondering generality": I was giving an "instructional league" clinic, a forty-five-minute lesson followed by forty-five minutes of observed doubles play. In the doubles play portion of the clinic, four ladies were in the middle of a good point, and both teams were in a one-up, one-back formation (one net person, one baseline person). I was watching from the net post when I saw the net person in front of me move back one step every time the ball was hit to her partner until, finally, she was standing at the serve line. Then it happened—the opposing baseline lady hit the ball right at her feet, which resulted in her hitting the ball into the net.

I asked her, "Why were you backing up?"

She said, "The ball was not coming to me, so I wondered if I was in the wrong position."

My response to her was, "It was because you were in the *right* place that no one wanted to hit it to you."

Her response gave me great insight into net players. She became a "wandering and wondering generality," wandering around, wondering if she was in the wrong place, so she moved back.

Do not be a wandering and wondering generality, be a "meaningful specific."

Practice with a Purpose; Play with a Passion.
—Unknown

No Brakes!

It was a rainy day in Largo, Florida, and some of the guys were sitting around the tennis shop waiting for the rain to stop. All of these members were former athletes; there was a catcher from the Major League Baseball Organization, a quarterback for Boston College, and an international cyclist. I was also there with the club owner and a head tennis pro. The owner of the club asked the former quarterback to tell a story about his college career. Then others in the room followed by telling stories of their careers—some funny, some inspiring.

The quarterback for Boston College started by telling a funny story from a big rivalry football game; then the Major League Baseball team catcher told a funny story from spring training; then the cyclist told an inspiring story with a poignant tennis meaning.

He had entered a race that was much like the Tour de France. He described events as he was riding this way: "The eventual winner and I were climbing a steep hill. We were close to each other, but my adversary was a second ahead. The two of us were leading the pack by, say, five or six seconds, and in cycling, that is a large margin. We reached the top and started downhill. Both of us were cruising fast down this hill that had many twists and turns. One turn had quite a sharp angle, and at that severe turn came the moment that defines the difference between a champion and a participant." He continued, "The winner saw the sharp turn, leaned into it, and didn't apply the brakes. I, and all the others, applied the brakes. That is why I finished second; I applied the brakes."

Every time you worry about making a mistake in a tennis match or are "too careful" or "guiding the ball," you are applying the brakes. From the cyclist's story, we learned the difference between winning and losing sometimes is as simple as playing with NO BRAKES!

"Give it all up, and you can have it all"

—Ram Dass

"Sometimes, Less Said Is Best Said" —Curly Davis

I would often travel to USTA national tournaments, and one was in Balboa Park in San Diego, California. It is a large tennis facility with enough courts to be able to run two tournaments at the same time. I was there for the USTA National Girls' sixteen and under, and a local wheelchair tournament was also going on.

I coached three players in National Girls', all with different personalities and approaches to preparing for a match. One was Courtney Allen, small in stature but big in heart; if you asked her to do something, she would try it, no questions asked. She also fought until the last point, never giving up. Sometimes, but not always, she would be greatly disappointed if she lost a match, which usually happened when she did not play to her potential. Another strength of hers was that she was a sponge when it came to learning the game and how to improve herself. She often followed me around, and as we stopped and watched a match, I told her my thoughts on the players' weaknesses and strengths.

Before the tournament started, I was on the practice court with three players, including Courtney. The girls were practicing with each other getting used to the speed of the courts, the surroundings, when a gentleman with a tennis racket and in a wheelchair came alongside our court and watched. Later, as I walked by him, we started talking, and I learned he was participating in the wheelchair event. We exchanged formalities, and I introduced him to the three girls. The man said to me, "Coach, I like the way you teach. Do you have time to work with my game and coach me? I'm not playing as well as I would like."

We arranged a time to hit later that day. It was a delight for me, not just to help him but to be a part of the courage he and all wheelchair players display. When we finished, I asked when he was scheduled to play in his tournament. It was about the same time that Courtney was scheduled to play, but I told him, "If I get a chance, I'll find time to come watch."

The next day came, and I warmed up Courtney and the others. Courtney went on for her match, but unfortunately, she did not play to her potential. She lost and came off the court in tears. Having been in this situation before with other players, and familiar with their personalities, I knew how and when to offer constructive criticism. Courtney was being hard on herself; I did not need to say anything at this time other than, "Let's go see how the wheelchair tournament is going."

We found the court, sat on a bench, and watched. Mind you, Courtney was still visibly upset, and I was still saying nothing. Courtney stopped her tears as we sat and waited for my thoughts on her match. Finally, she looked around, saw the man from yesterday playing, and saw the other wheelchair participants. She looked at me and said, "I get it!"

I acknowledged her and said, "Yes . . . it's disappointing you lost, but look at the courage that's being displayed out there."

> *A smart person knows what to say. A wise person knows whether or not to say it.*
>
> —Unknown

Watch What You Say

An early lesson in my teaching career, between high school and going off to college, I had a summer job teaching tennis in the Louisville Public Parks. Louisville has a great public parks system—large parks with walking and jogging trails, and many sports fields and events, tennis being just one of them. I was assigned to go to a different park each morning, plus a different park in the afternoon. It was a wonderful way for me to see if I really wanted to make teaching tennis my career.

One morning, I was assigned to Shawnee Park (most parks in Louisville were named after Native American tribes that were indigenous in the area). I had a group of five girls from the ages of six to twelve. They were lined up across the baseline, spaced out so they wouldn't hit each other when they swung their rackets. I stood a yard or two in front of them facing the net and taught the basic forehand stroke.

My cues were, "Turn, take your racket back to the fence," "Step forward," etc. To emphasize the racket preparation, I repeated, "Turn, take your racket back to the fence." As I turned around to make sure they were all taking their racket back, one girl was taking my instructional cue literally and was walking back toward the fence, carrying her racket back to the fence!

I learned to watch my phrasing.

The text has disappeared under the interpretation.
—Friedrich Nietzsche

Clark Kent or Superman?

Every serious tennis player dreams of being on the professional tennis circuit, and I was no different. I was a twenty-three-year-old, teaching pro in St. Petersburg, Florida, when I learned of a pro tournament coming to Orlando. You may not know that, before every pro tournament, there is a "qualifying tournament," a.k.a. "qualies." The finalist of this tournament receives a spot in the main tournament. Many players go from qualies to qualies to try to break through; these players are referred to as "rabbits," chasing after the "big boys."

I entered in the Orlando qualies, along with 127 other rabbits, and was to play on the first day of the tournament. I thought I would give myself an advantage over my opponent by wearing a tennis shirt that had a Superman emblem on it. I wore a sweater over the shirt, so my opponent would not know the surprise I had in store for him!

I was waiting for my match when I spotted a local reporter for the *Orlando Sentinel*. Never passing up an opportunity to receive "press," I went over to the reporter and lifted my sweater to reveal my Superman shirt! He pulled me over to the nearest phone booth (they still had them then), and asked to take two pictures, one with the sweater on, then with the sweater off, showing the emblem. Soon after we finished with the photos and interview, I was called to go onto the stadium court for my match.

My opponent's name was Jose Betancur from South America. We greeted each other and walked onto the court with around one hundred spectators. I was still wearing the sweater as we warmed up. Then the time came to make the big reveal to psyche him out. I went over to my chair and pulled off the sweater, revealing it to the spectators and to Jose. I raised my arms in the air, as a muscle builder would do. The spectators laughed but Jose looked perplexed, then he looked toward his coach and asked a question in Spanish. The coach interpreted his question and said to me in his Spanish accent, "He does not understand. What is this on your shirt?" The joke was on *me*! Being from South America, he did not know about Superman and was completely unfamiliar with the emblem. Well, it went downhill for me after that— Jose won the match 6–4, 6–1.

Wait . . . it gets worse! The next day I was sitting in my hotel room preparing to drive back to St. Petersburg when the maid knocked on the door. I told her to come in. She looked at me and started speaking Spanish in an overly excited way! I informed her I did not speak Spanish, and she immediately ran out of the room then came back with a newspaper in one hand and a pen in the other. She opened it to the sports section. I was perplexed until I saw a large photograph of myself on the front page. She wanted my autograph under the article titled, "HE THOUGHT HE WAS SUPERMAN . . . BUT WASN'T." My touring pro dream came to an end, reinforcing my dream to be a teaching pro, where my "heart" has always been.

> *Believe in your heart that you're meant to live a life full of passion, purpose, magic, and miracles.*
> —Roy T. Bennett, *The Light in the Heart*

Meeting Willie Mays, the "Say Hey Kid"

I was in Treasure Island, Florida, in the mid-1970s, teaching tennis and single. The season was spring, and baseball spring training camps had started in the Tampa Bay area. Many pro baseball teams trained out of the Tampa Bay area. One such team was the from New York. I had a first date with a lovely lady, and I was trying to impress her by wearing a white polyester sports jacket with red and blue pinstripes, a navy-blue turtleneck, and white polyester slacks (don't laugh, remember, it was the '70s; polyester was in). I took her to my favorite restaurant, The Fog-Cutter—my friend Dick Gold owned it. Dick met us at the door, where he greeted me with a big "Hello, Curly" while he was picking his teeth. Dick then said, "Sorry, I'm picking my teeth; I'm having dinner with many of the Major League baseball team members, their wives, and Willie Mays." Dick sat us down, and I ordered a bottle of wine.

The Fog-Cutter boasted of a new restaurant item called the salad bar. I excused myself to my date and went to the salad bar. As I walked over, I noticed that Dick was now sitting down with all the New York Mets, their wives, and there was Willie Mays, sitting at the head of the table.

While I was selecting items from the salad bar, I heard Dick Gold say behind me to the table, "That's Curly Davis. He's a tennis pro in town."

One of the Mets' wives said, "I'd like to meet him because I want to take lessons while I'm in town." I heard this, but I could not just turn around and say I was eavesdropping; I had to wait on Dick to call me over.

While their conversation went on, I selected items from the salad bar. I was placing butter on my plate when Dick called me over. I took one step and realized I had taken the salad bar's butter fork. I excused myself, went back to the salad bar to replace the butter fork, and when I did, I had taken the butter fork by the prongs, unbeknownst to me, and placed it back on the bar.

I turned around and Dick introduced me first to the Say Hey Kid, Willie Mays. I put out my hand to give him a firm handshake, looking him straight in the eye. His hand hit mine, and then we both realized . . . I had butter all over my hand! I panicked, wiping my hand down the front of my white slacks, leaving a yellow stripe down the front them!

I went back to the table where my date was and took the wine bottle, placed it to my lips and just chugged it! Me and my yellow stripe on my pants.

> *Embarrassing is the moment when you realize that person wasn't waving at you.*
> —Curly Davis

A View From Across the Net

Hammerin' Hank and a Chorus of Boos

Saddlebrook Resort often wanted a presence at significant tennis tournaments. I was selected to be their representative at two: the Legg-Mason—now known as the Citi Open in Washington, DC—and the Verizon Tennis Challenge—the Atlanta Open. Saddlebrook had a booth at each of these tournaments, and, in addition, I presented an on-court stroke demo at the stadium before the featured match of the evening.

This particular evening in Atlanta, I presented my demo on the stadium court before an audience of two thousand. I was demon16tarting the volley, and I had pulled a lady from the audience to help with the demo. As I was talking into the microphone, explaining the volley stroke, I spotted a childhood hero of mine stepping into the stands—baseball legend and Hall of Famer Hank Aaron, a.k.a. "Hammerin' Hank."

Without thinking about it, and as a child would do, I blurted out, "Hammerin' Hank Aaron!" I forgot what I was doing and became a child again.

> *For in every adult there dwells the child that was, and in every child there lies the adult that will be.*
> —John Connolly

In the second story, I was at the tournament in Washington, DC, getting ready to go on court to perform the demo. The tournament official came up to me and asked me to announce that the number-one seed, Michael Chang, the person the audience was here to see, had pulled out of the tournament and wouldn't be playing that night.

I said, "Sending me out to the wolves?" However, I did as they asked; I informed the crowd and received a chorus of "boos." I went on with my demo and watched as 50 percent of the crowd left the stadium court. It is a very humbling experience, being booed.

> *I understand the fans, I respect them. I'll accept the whistling and booing. It's up to me to transform that all into applause.*
> —Leonardo Bonucci

Lessons in Winning and Losing

I was a junior in high school, and I had made it to the Kentucky State High School Championships, playing against Tom Copper, my nemesis. Tom was a great talent; he was the youngest in a family of accomplished tennis players. He also had the advantage of living across the street from tennis courts, so he had older brothers and tennis courts right there whenever he wanted to play. Tom had never been beaten in his high school tennis career. He had won the Kentucky State High School Championship his freshman and sophomore years, and now he, too, was in his junior year.

We had played many times, and to the best of my recollection, he had beaten me more than I beat him. It was always very frustrating since I worked hard year-round, while he played his tennis only in the spring and summer and switched to basketball in the winter.

We met in the Kentucky State High School Championship finals in Seneca Park, in Louisville, Kentucky. I was playing well, and so was Tom, a sign of a good tennis match. We were on a clay court with ten open courts around us—no one else could play during our match, so there would be no distractions. A crowd of maybe one hundred spectators, including my dad, mom, my high school tennis coach (who was a football coach and, admittedly, knew nothing about tennis), and my actual tennis coach/instructor, Gustavo Palafox, who played for his home country in a team event.

I can see it to this very day, where everyone was seated: My dad sat front and center; my mother, the nervous type, was farther away, pacing back and forth, smoking her cigarettes; my tennis coach/instructor was sitting beside my dad; and my high school coach was chain-smoking and pacing up and down the right sideline.

We played well, and the first set went back and forth; I won 6–4. This boosted my confidence going into the second set, and I broke his serve on the first game, then held serve to get a quick lead: 2–0. Tom served and held to make it 2–1. I held serve to make it 3–1. Tom held serve for 3–2; I then held to go up to 4–2.

I could see Tom's body language was not positive, almost resigned to the possibility of me beating him for the first time in a high school tennis match. Tom was serving, and I had a breakpoint (40–30). If I broke, I would go up to 5–2 and serve for the match and title.

Tom hit his first serve into the net. It gave me a great opportunity, a second serve at breakpoint. I moved inside the baseline to add pressure. Tom served, and it landed six inches long . . . I hit it back over the baseline on Tom's side.

Tom asked, "Were you playing that?" I knew it was long; I saw the ball mark, but my response was, "I was playing it."

An "oh" was heard from the spectators. The score went back to deuce, and Tom held, then broke my serve 4–4. I thought more about the call I did not make than the moment in the match. Tom went on to beat me, 6–4, 6–4, 6–2.

After the match, Tom said, "I could not believe you called my serve good." Frankly, I could not either. As I came off the court, my father was the first to greet me with his hand out and a smile, congratulating me on a good match, then my high school coach and tennis coach congratulated me. Tom went on to an undefeated high school career.

In wins, and particularly in losses, there are lessons. The lesson I learned in this loss was:

"Don't cheat your opponent, but don't cheat yourself."
—Curly Davis

Another Story From My Kentucky High School Championship Finals

Every sport has two sayings that often contradict one another. They are:

1. Never change a winning game plan
2. Always keep your opponent off-balance

The prevailing wisdom is that once you start winning at your sport, keep doing what you're doing to keep winning. Maintain an "If it ain't broke, don't fix it" attitude. But if you keep doing what is beating your challenger, aren't they going to catch on? So, you change to keep your opponent off-balance, and you move away from a winning game plan. The following story illustrates this.

I described my Kentucky High School Championship match in the previous story. I was winning with short-landing slice backhands that exited the sidelines, many outright winners. My opponent was bewildered about how to counter that tactic. However, as the match progressed, I thought I'd keep him "off-balance" by hitting my backhand down the line. That tactic worked for some situations, but I eventually moved away from the wide-angle slice backhand. I moved away from rule number one in sports: *Never change a winning game plan*. As mentioned in the earlier story, I lost the match.

> *Never change a winning game; always change a losing one.*
>
> —Bill Tilden

What Lines Are We Playing?

I was in Hungary, in a small town called Pécs, for a satellite pro tournament. Pro tournaments have different levels: Tier 1 is what you view on TV, followed by the Challenger level going down to the satellite level. Typically, the satellite level is players just starting their pro career with no ranking or ranked low on the world ranking.

I was there because I was coaching a German ATP player named Michael Gardermann; he was ranked #1,033 globally. Michael was a good player with dreams of making it big, but his work effort was lacking; fortunately, his family was sponsoring him (*sponsoring* meaning paying for his travel expenses as well as my coaching and travel expenses). The tournament was on red-clay courts, with the lines placed down with chalk, like a baseball chalk line. Every three or five games, the maintenance crew would run out on changeovers (players changing ends of the court) and re-chalk the court since players would slide across the line to retrieve a shot from the opponent, thereby erasing the line.

Tournament matches started at eight a.m., going through the entire day, so by noon, the chalk lines had been replaced many times. What made it so interesting and funny, the maintenance crew enjoyed drinking wine between having to re-chalk the courts.

When the afternoon match started, there were many different lines on the court: the original lines followed by the "not-so-intoxicated" lines to the "drunk" lines, which were up to an inch off from the original. There were arguments heard from all the players as they were playing, "Which lines are we playing? The original or drunk lines?" An argument you won't see on TV!

Show me someone who has done something worthwhile, and I'll show you someone who has overcome adversity.
—Lou Holtz

Talking About the Weather

Since coaching and training Michael, I lived in Germany for a month or two leading up to tournaments. Because of my time there, I could pick up some communication skills, limited speaking, and limited understanding of the German language.

While at the same satellite tournament in Hungary, the tournament site had lower back fences behind the courts so spectators and coaches could stand behind the fence to view the matches. Also, the nature of satellite-level tournaments, players and coaches were hungry for wins, and "bending" the rules was the norm. It was understood that most players were playing for "food money," as stated in the previous story. Michael was fortunate not to have to worry about playing for "food money" like most other players did.

Michael was playing against an Italian player, during the match, I was standing next to a gentleman who turned out to be the coach of the Italian player. Every changeover, the gentleman next to me would call his player over and speak to him, in Italian—a rule infraction. After several times, I looked around for the roaming umpire, but they were not anywhere near. I had had enough, so next changeover, I called over Michael, and we started talking in English, while next to me was the Italian coach talking to his charge.

Both of us were talking strategy and tactics. But there was a roaming umpire around; he came over to me and said, "Warning: coaching!"

I stopped and looked at the umpire and then back at the Italian coach and player, and they had not stopped talking. I asked, "Coaching?! What do you think they are doing?" while pointing at the Italian coach and player. "Talking about the weather?!"

The umpire's response was, "I don't speak Italian."

This infuriated me, making for my tart response: "Don't

penalize us because you understand English!" He went on to inform me I still had a warning for coaching.

I asked, "Do you speak German?"

He said, "No," so I started to coach Michael in German while the umpire was there. The umpire verbally came at me again and said, "If you're coaching, your player will have a point penalty against him."

I said, "Not to worry, and we are talking about the weather just like these two," and pointed at the Italian coach and player. They never did stop talking through the umpire's and my conversation.

> *When things do not go your way, remember that every challenge—every adversity—contains within it the seeds of opportunity and growth.*
> —Roy T. Bennett

Brian Baker—The King of the Comebacks

Brian Baker is a former touring pro. One of the highlights of his career was in 2012 when he reached the fourth round of Wimbledon.

Let me tell you my story with Brian.

Several years ago, the USTA started a "zonal competition." They gathered the best twelve-and-under tennis players from each zone in the country for a team competition. This competition was unusual in that coaching was allowed by the coaches designated for each section. I was gratified to be chosen by the Southern Tennis Association as one of these coaches.

My team consisted of many good players, including twelve-year-old Brian Baker, who played number one singles for our team. In every match, Brian started well, winning the first set by hitting smart shots, but then he fell in "love" with his drop shot and would try it on almost every point. The opponent would invariably catch on and make his adjustment. By the second set, the opponent was anticipating them and ready to run down the drop shots, taking away Brian's winning shot.

I informed Brian that he tried the "dropper" too often and it was too predictable, but he didn't change. Don't get me wrong, he had an excellent drop shot, but it was too easy to read. I used a different approach and asked Brian, "What is your favorite car?"

He answered, "Ferrari."

I said, "Okay, so your Ferrari has several different gears that you can choose. You are stuck in first gear by playing the drop shot so often. So, try shifting gears and hitting the ball a little faster, and now and then shift to a lower gear—meaning your drop shot." He understood my comparison and stopped using the drop shot so much.

Many years passed, and Brian went on to great tennis results and turned pro. He trained at Saddlebrook Resort, where I worked. We had a wonderful conversation on the golf cart as we drove to the tennis courts one day.

He asked, "Do you remember me?"

I said, "Of course," and we laughed about his love affair with the drop shot. Then he said, "I never forgot your coaching advice, using the Ferrari shifting gears analogy; it has stayed with me."

Brian had many injuries throughout his tennis career, but he always put his head down and made numerous comebacks from those injuries.

"Success travels in the company of very hard work. There is no trick, no easy way."

—John Wooden

ONE TOO MANY ONES: MY COMPETITIVENESS

I have been playing tennis since I was five years old, going on to play in tournaments both as a youngster and now as a senior. Today, I still enjoy playing competitively.

Don't get me wrong, I am highly competitive when it comes to my tennis. My doubles partner and close friend in the sixty-five-and-overs is Hugh Sawyer. Hugh has a little more time and desire to work on his game and follows the results of tournaments more than I do.

Hugh and I played in a doubles tournament back in my hometown and at my home club, the Louisville Boat Club. I was looking forward to going back home to Louisville to see family and friends, plus playing at the same club where I grew up and played all my junior tennis matches.

Hugh and I had a good tournament and, on this occasion, we won the tournament. Time went by, and Hugh called me up to give me some good news: Hugh said, "With our winning the Boat Club tournament, we are now ranked number eleven in the nation in sixty-five-and-overs!" I enjoyed hearing that news, but my competitiveness came out, with me saying, "That's one too many ones for me." I guess no matter how old an athlete gets, they will always be driven.

My only competition is myself.

—Unknown

WE ALL MUST BE HUMBLED NOW AND THEN

As you may or may not know, I have written two books on tennis. I did a book tour of several cities to promote them, one in my hometown of Louisville, Kentucky. For this tour, I flew from Tampa to Louisville with a stopover in Atlanta. One of the passengers boarding in Atlanta was another Louisvillian much more famous than I: the People's Champion, the Greatest, Muhammed Ali! The buzz and the staring were evident.

In Louisville, my book signing was scheduled for the next day at two p.m. but I was instructed to be there a half hour ahead of schedule. I duly showed up at the bookstore at 1:30 p.m., and what do I see but a line out the door! I thought, *WOW! All of my friends and former clients showed up to buy and have me sign their book"* I was feeling rather good about myself.

You can guess where I am going with this... Yes, Muhammed Ali had the book signing before mine at the same bookstore, and they were there to see him!

Me? I ended up with three people to see me; most certainly, the line was not "out the door." Every now and then, we all must be humbled.

Humility will open more doors than arrogance ever will.
—Zig Ziglar

Jack Nicholas vs. Me

Tennis professionals often have wealthy, celebrity clients. One such client (who will remain anonymous to protect his privacy) called me one day to arrange a series of lessons for his wife as a birthday gift. He did not ask the price, but I apologetically explained to him that the facility was under new management and said that, in my estimation, they had raised the rates to unreasonably expensive levels. He replied, "Money is *not* an issue." We finished our conversation and I waited for his wife to receive her gift; after a week or two, her assistant called to arrange the lessons.

While picking up balls at the end of the first lesson, we engaged in small talk to get to know one another. I found out that she had gone to the University of Kentucky, my state university, and we knew many people in common. Further in our conversation, I mentioned, "It was so nice of your husband to give you these tennis lessons as a birthday gift." She said, "Yes, it was."

She went on to tell me that her husband was a *big* golf enthusiast and played in many of the pro-am golf events on the PGA Tour. She also mentioned that her husband had had a birthday a few weeks earlier.

I was curious. "If you don't mind me asking, what was your gift to him?"

Her response floored me: "As I told you, he's a golf enthusiast so I got him eighteen holes with Jack Nicholas!" Of course, my response was, "He's playing eighteen holes of golf with *Jack Nicholas* and you received tennis lessons with me?! You certainly got the short end of the gifts here!"

Every gift from a friend is a wish for your happiness.
—Richard Bach

Pete Sampras's Weakness

Michael Chang was in his post-match interview after Pete Sampras's all-around tennis game soundly beat him. A reporter asked Michael, "What is Pete's weakness?"

Michael thought a bit and then responded, "I don't think he can cook."

"A good laugh makes any interview, or any conversation, so much better."
— Barbara Walters.

Most Famous Tennis Quote

For years, Jimmy Connors "owned" Vitas Gerulaitis, having beaten him *sixteen times in a row*. But in 1980, Vitas and Jimmy played for the seventeenth time, and Vitas finally was the victor.

In the post-match interview, a reporter asked Vitas, "What was the difference this time?"

Vitas responded, *"Nobody beats Vitas Gerulaitis seventeen times in a row."*

It might be the most famous quote in tennis history.

You may encounter many defeats, but you must not be defeated. In fact, it may be necessary to encounter the defeats, so you can know who you are, what you can rise from, how you can still come out of it.
— Maya Angelou

I Know, Don't Tell Me

All I have in teaching this wonderful game are words—words to paint a picture of what one has done wrong, if there is to be any improvement. Without this, how can I possibly assist in improving your game? When teaching tennis, the words "I know, don't tell me" push me over the edge because it completely muzzles me.

Here is a story to illustrate: I was giving a lesson to an intermediate-level player in Louisville. As I instructed her, she started with the "I know, don't tell me what I did wrong" statement. As I mentioned, it irritates me, but I kept my thoughts to myself and kept on instructing her, though she sulkily repeated "I know, don't tell me" throughout the lesson.

Toward the end of the lesson, she asked if I would look at her serve. She came to my side of the court, where the ball basket was, and while I watched her serve, she made the same statement. Even when I saw her hit a perfect serve, I responded with silence, crickets...nothing. She asked me, "Aren't you going to tell me what a good serve it was?" I was finally able to counter her statement by saying, "I figured you already knew since you seem to know everything else!"

When taking a lesson, know that it is a *partnership* between you and the instructor, and on many occasions, all we have are words to illuminate our teaching points.

> *It is what we know already that often prevents us from learning.*
>
> —Claude Bernard

Don't Lift the Fig Leaf

I had the privilege of traveling to many places while I was coaching good junior players. One such player, let us call him Bobby, was the most talented player I ever coached. I would explain the body's movement and the mechanics of a stroke *once*, and he could do it *flawlessly*. He would listen and trust what I told him; in short, he would do what I told him with no debate.

Bobby was short and skinny, with brown hair and large ears that stuck out. When embarrassed, Bobby's ears would turn bright red! He was quite the personality. He loved to smile and was an adventurer.

Those unfamiliar with winter junior tournaments may not know they are usually scheduled during school holiday breaks—Thanksgiving, Christmas, Spring Break, etc. There are many tennis tournaments for nationally ranked juniors, one such being the National Boys' fourteen and under USTA Indoor Championships, played in Chicago during the Thanksgiving holiday.

When Bobby and I were in Chicago for the tournament, he played on Thanksgiving Day and lost, so he did not have to play the next day. Since we were staying downtown, we walked down Michigan Avenue to see the city, which was teeming with Christmas shoppers. We went to the mall and into a popular toy store, again crammed with shoppers. Bobby and I wandered around and ended up in the back of the store. Standing right in the middle of the floor was a life-size stuffed, naked mannequin with only a fig leaf over where his "private parts" would be. On the floor by the dummy's right foot was a sign, stating, "DON'T LIFT THE FIG LEAF." WELL?!

You do not tell a man not to do something because he will always want to disobey and do it (I guess it's in our DNA). Since I wanted to lift the fig leaf but did not have the courage, I instructed Bobby to go over and lift the fig leaf. He took on the task and slowly started walking over to the mannequin. He looked back several times to check for assurance, and I nodded an encouraging "go ahead" each time.

Meanwhile, a group of "wannabe" onlookers had gathered to see the results. (I say "wannabe" because they wanted to do it themselves but, like me, did not have the courage—only *unlike* me, they did not have a student to instruct to do it for them.) Bobby reached the mannequin, and with one final look back, he reached for the fig leaf. I again nodded my approval. With a shaking hand, he lifted the fig leaf! It was *wired*!

Sirens went off, a spotlight shined down on him, and a disco ball lit up and started turning! Bobby came running back to my side, smiling, and his big ears were throbbing a bright red! The onlookers were laughing, and I was too! It makes me smile just writing about it.

Adventure is not outside man; it is within.
—George Eliot

Somebody Tooted

This Bobby story happened the following year from the story above. Bobby and I were in Boston for the Boys' USTA sixteen and under National Indoor Championships at Thanksgiving time. Some indoor courts were covered by an air structure—a.k.a. a "bubble"—which is kept up by air being pumped into it. It's common for clubs to have a bubble because they can be taken down in summer, unlike permanent indoor court structures, which remain enclosed year-round.

Bobby had never played in a bubble, however; the disadvantage of bubbles is that noise carries and amplifies—it is easy to think you are hitting the ball ridiculously hard and even try to hit it harder than you should. So, the day before the tournament, I purposely signed up for a practice court there so that he could experience the sound. There were three practice courts and one court with temporary bleachers for coaches, parents, and fans.

On three courts, players were practicing for the tournament; Bobby and I were on one of them. The bleachers were filled with parents or players waiting to practice. I was hitting with Bobby, everyone else was hitting, and it was *loud* in the bubble, but suddenly, and without coordination, all courts stopped hitting at the same time... then it happened, someone ripped a fart that echoed throughout the bubble! Everyone started to laugh and look around—and there stood Bobby... smiling, laughing, bright red ears throbbing away; I knew then who cut the fart!

Life is too short to be serious all the time, so if you can't laugh at yourself, call me ... I'll laugh at you.
—Unknown

Someone Just Blinked

In every hotly contested tennis match, there is a point when the momentum changes. Here is what happened to me:

I was playing doubles in the finals of a local tournament in Kentucky. Our opponent was a well-seasoned team that had played together for many years and thus knew each other's game very well. My partner and I had played some tournaments together, but many fewer than the other team.

It was a close match—each team had won a set, and we were playing out the third set. We got to six all and about to start the seven-point tiebreaker when I looked at my partner and said, "Now it's whoever blinks, loses."

The tiebreak score was close; we were up 3–2, and then it happened—my partner threw up a weak lob that was going to land close to the net. One of the opponents came charging in to smash it away, but he proceeded to hit the ball into the bottom of the net! I smiled at my partner and said, "Somebody just blinked." We went on to win 7–2 in the tiebreak and won the match.

Next close match you play, look for your opportunity to extend your lead or to come from behind.

> *Opportunities are like sunrises. If you wait too long, you miss them.*
>
> —William Arthur Ward

I Didn't Throw My Racket!

Many enthusiastic tennis fans and spectators may not realize that every time a pro smashes or throws their racket (racket abuse), curses (verbal obscenity), or berates an umpire or linesperson (unsportsmanlike conduct), there is a corresponding monetary fine, such as $250 for dropping a racket, $500 for throwing the racket, etc. One such time is a funny story.

Frank Hammond, one of the first chair umpires in the game of tennis, was officiating a match between Illie Nastase and another player. Illie was one of the first "bad boys" of tennis; you never knew what Illie would do in a match—sometimes funny, occasionally nasty gestures, or antics, earning him the nickname "Nasty Nastase."

During the match, after Illie missed a shot and the racket left his hand, the following conversation took place between Frank and Illie:

Frank: "Racket abuse, Mr. Nastase."

Illie: "What racket abuse?"

Frank: "You threw your racket."

Illie: "I didn't throw my racket. I dropped my racket!"

Frank: "What's the difference?"

Straight-faced, Illie immediately replied, "250 dollars." (He was referring to the difference between the fine for throwing, $500, and the fine for dropping, $250.)

At that point, even Frank Hammond had to break out laughing.

Don't Hide and Seek!

It was 1973, and I was a young teaching pro in Treasure Island, Florida, teaching at the Treasure Island Tennis and Yacht Club. Tennis was in the midst of a boom—everyone was playing tennis. The tennis match, "Battle of the Sexes," between Billie Jean King and Bobby Riggs had just happened on prime-time television, with over fifty million viewing nationwide. Everyone wanted to play tennis and take tennis lessons; times were busy for tennis instructors.

It was a beautiful Saturday on Florida's west coast. I had tennis lessons scheduled all morning. All twenty-three courts at the club were in use, and I was the one farthest from the clubhouse. Don Kaiser was the head pro and my mentor. As a professional tennis instructor, he took me under his wing and gave me guidance on what to say and do. Don stressed that when teaching a beginner, never let them see you laugh at their mistakes. A beginner is very self-conscious during the lesson, and if you laugh, it will only make them embarrassed and anxious. To this day, I obey that lesson because Don was one of the most popular teaching pros in the area.

My ten a.m. lesson was one such beginner—a tall attractive woman taking her first-ever tennis lesson, one of the many wishing to learn tennis. She was dressed in a newly purchased tennis outfit and had a borrowed tennis racket; she looked the part. I did my best to set her at ease by telling her I expected her to swing and miss or hit many off the frame of the racket—anything to make her feel that I had seen it before, which I have.

I went to my ball cart, which holds two hundred balls for lessons, to get another handful of balls. I can hold six, which allows carrying on a rally without stopping to get another ball, thus slowing down the lesson. As expected, she would swing and miss and I would encourage her by saying, "I still swing and miss every day, even after playing for nineteen years" (which was true at that time). She continued swinging, missing, and hitting the frame of the racket, with the ball ricocheting off somewhere, up in the air, off to the left or to the right. She started to hit a few back between the swinging and missing, or "foul-tipping," still a normal occurrence.

I needed another handful of balls, so I went back to the ball cart, got out six more. I fed a ball to her, and it hit off the bottom part of her racket frame. The ball bounced off the ground and went all the way up between her legs! Having deflected a ball before, she looked up to her left, then up to her right, then she looked at me with a "where'd it go?" look.

Now, I knew where the ball went, but Don, my mentor, had never taught me to inform a lesson-taker, particularly a lady, when the ball is located in a . . . shall we say, "sensitive area." I was about to say something to her, when she took one step, and threw her arms up in an "I don't know where it is" gesture. When she did that, the ball fell from between her legs, causing a chain of events: she looked down, saw the ball, and then realized where it had been. She looked up at me aghast, but I immediately turned my back and went back to gather more balls from the cart. Really, I was turning away so she could not see me laugh! I was on my own!

The old hidden ball trick!

"Being embarrassed means you are human, and we like you better for it."

—Nick Morgan

A View From Across the Net

ANDRE AGASSI AND HEE HAW

In the '70s, a TV show titled *Hee Haw* remained in production into the 1990s. *Hee Haw* was a country-style take on *Rowan & Martin's Laugh-In*, a hugely popular show. *Hee Haw* was popular throughout the South since its humor was directed at and for southern and/or rural audiences.

Andre had just made a crossover from tennis star—tennis enthusiasts would recognize him as a super star, where people will recognize a player even though they are not a tennis enthusiast. With that new super stardom, Andre was requesting security wherever he went so he could protect himself and his entourage. He was playing in a tournament in Cincinnati, where he would fly into the Greater Cincinnati Airport in Covington, Kentucky. His arrival was at two a.m. on a Sunday morning.

His plane arrived, and a lady from the tournament was there to greet him as he disembarked. The lady welcomed him, whereupon Andre looked around and asked, "Where's my security I requested?" The lady responded, "Mr. Agassi, it's two o'clock on a Sunday morning; you're in northern Kentucky. Unless you've been on *Hee Haw* in the last two weeks . . . nobody's going to know who you are!"

"What is important is (to know) what is not important!"
— Abhijit Kar Gupta

A Career Lesson

It was a rainy day in Louisville, Kentucky, and I was a young tennis pro at the Louisville Country Club. Knowing I wanted to make a career in tennis, I sought the guidance of the golf director at the club. He had been the golf pro at the Louisville Country Club for a long time and was well respected in the area. Being at any country club for a length of time is quite an accomplishment because the life span at a country club is an average of two years, so he must have been doing something right!

I asked the golf director, "I wish to make tennis a professional career. Do you have any advice?" His answer has stuck with me and has served me well, plus has come up on several occasions" *"Make every member feel like they're your best friend, but never forget . . . they are the member."*

An illustration of this career lesson came up a few years later. In another state, I was at a club as the tennis pro and went out for dinner and drinks with members, a regular occurrence. The dinner and socializing went on into the wee hours of the evening, with much drinking, laughing, and friendship.

The next day I was at the club and the friends I had just "partied" with a few hours earlier came into the pro shop for a court they had booked, and I forgot to put them down. I had no court for them; they became quite agitated with me and started yelling at me for my forgetfulness. I was surprised because we were joking, socializing, etc. the night before and now they were yelling. They made me remember the lesson the country club golf director had given me early in my career—they were exercising their member rights.

> *Being professional is just really clearly the way to go and helps you on the road to longevity.*
> —Amanda Seyfried

Momma's Gonna Hear 'Bout This

It was a busy Saturday morning at the Indian Springs Tennis and Yacht Club in Largo, Florida. Members and guests filled all thirteen courts. I was the assistant pro, conducting a junior clinic on the middle court, designated the teaching court so the pro could see the comings and goings of the members. The juniors, aged five to ten years old, included six-year-old Johnny and his sister, ten-year-old Jennifer.

Johnny often got my notice because he did not pay attention or play friendly with the others. Every time I had to reprimand him, his sister, always right behind Johnny, would yell, "Momma's gonna hear 'bout this!"

I would say, "Johnny, leave Billy alone." And Jennifer would echo, "Momma's gonna hear 'bout this!"

"Johnny, quit using your tennis racket like a sword; you could hurt someone with it." Jennifer would chime in, "Momma's gonna hear 'bout this!" In short, he was a handful, and Jennifer was annoying.

Toward the end of the clinic, the kids played a game of "orange ball." I would set up a ball machine with all yellow tennis balls except one orange ball. I set the ball machine at a slow speed to allow the players time to hit the ball. Each kid would hit until they missed. The kid who was up when the orange ball shot out of the machine and could hit it safely over the net and inside the lines won a soda. I was standing on the other side by the ball machine informing the juniors if the ball landed in or out. I would yell "Next" if the ball landed out. The purpose of the drill was to encourage consistency rather than hitting "home runs" as most boys tried to do.

The game was going well, but I noticed that these young players trying to hit the ball would swing and miss more often than not. When they swung and missed, the ball would hit the next person standing in line. I stopped the ball machine and yelled from across the court, "Make sure your line isn't right behind the hitter; stand to the side of the hitter. That way, you don't get hit by the missed ball."

That worked for a little while, but the line worked its way behind the hitter again. Johnny was next in line; the hitter swung and missed, and it hit Johnny, right in the crotch. Johnny bent over in pain. I suddenly stopped the ball machine and called from across the court, "Make sure you stand *beside* the hitter, so you don't get hit by the ball."

Johnny yelled back at me, "I was, and still got hit right in the dick!"

A roar of laughter came up from the surrounding courts, all running over to see which kid said it. Johnny's sister started back in on him, saying, "OH! Momma's gonna hear 'bout this. Momma's gonna hear 'bout this!"

By then, Johnny had had enough of her. He wheeled around, got up in her face, and yelled, "SHUT UP!"

I couldn't have said it better.

"I wish more people were fluent in silence."

—Unknown

Kicking the Cactus

Often, colleges will include other sporting events during a football "bowl" to ramp up the media frenzy. One such was the Copper Bowl Tennis Tournament in Tucson, Arizona. It was held at a hotel with fifteen tennis courts that were only a short walk away, along a cactus-lined path.

I was coaching a group of juniors, ranging from twelve to seventeen years old, most of whom were playing their matches the first day of the tournament. One was a twelve-year-old boy who played and lost, unfortunately. As is my custom, I talked to him after the match and I found out that he was terribly upset. After our talk, he said he was going back to the room. I had to stay at the tennis court because I had other juniors playing then or about to go on court.

But as the young, dejected player walked back on the trail lined with cacti, I kept a watchful eye on him. His disappointment showed when he stopped, looked at a cactus, and then reared back his leg to kick it. I saw this and started to warn him, but... too late—he swung his leg forward with a mighty force. As I was yelling and running toward him, his leg rammed the cactus, and he started screaming in pain. I got there a second later and began the long, slow, painful process of pulling out all of the cactus needles embedded in his leg.

To this day, I cannot needle him about this (pun intended).

Mark My Words!

As tennis director at Saddlebrook Resort in Tampa (a world-renowned tennis destination), it was my duty to offer a stroke demo every morning. On this particular morning, I was demonstrating volleys, from grip to stroke, to a large group of Japanese tennis enthusiasts. Luckily, Saddlebrook has a Japanese interpreter on its impressive staff.

I was on court demonstrating the volley and stopping only for the interpreter to translate what I had just said. When I finished my demo, one of the Japanese campers posed a question through the interpreter: "On the volley grip, you mentioned the index finger had to be a little separate from the other fingers. How much space should there be between the index finger and the rest of the fingers?"

Flippantly, I threw out a figure of one-quarter inch, and the interrupter translated. Then to my amazement, I watched as the player who had asked the question walked over to his racket bag, pulled out a ruler, and measured and marked on his grip one-quarter inch from his index finger to the other fingers.

At the time I thought, *I better watch what I say; these tennis enthusiasts take it as the law!*

Martina Hingis: A Great Sense of Humor

Saddlebrook Resort in Florida has always attracted many top touring pros. One such player was Martina Hingis, who bought a home there just as she was in the finals of the French Open. (She has since sold it).

Martina was playing against Steffi Graff and was favored to win, but Steffi was her great self. She hit many slice backhands; the ball stayed close to the ground after it bounced, which forced Martina to hit up. This allowed Steffi to run around her backhand and blast a forehand. To compound Steffi's good play, the French crowd started to boo and even cheered against Martina. This upset Martina, so much so that when Steffi won the match, Martina didn't want to wait for the trophy presentation; her mother insisted she stay on the court. In short, it was pretty frustrating for Martina.

Fast forward to Wimbledon, where Martina was again one of the favorites to win, but she had a "hangover" from her play at the French Open and lost in the first round.

Her agent contacted Saddlebrook Resort and requested two cases of all the major tennis-ball manufacturers, and a ball machine that would oscillate, throw the balls up to 100 mph, and place topspin or slice on the ball. All had to be delivered within one week; we made it happen.

When Martina and her mother arrived, I explained the ball machine. I was standing behind it with the remote control, Martina was on the right, and her mother was on the left. I demonstrated how the ball machine would do everything they wanted—100 mph, oscillate, topspin, and slice. When Martina saw the slice the ball machine put out, she asked to see it again. I said, "Sure," and pushed the remote to make it demonstrate the slice again. It did. Martina immediately walked to the front of the ball machine, bent over to the hole where the ball came out, and asked, "Steffi . . . are you in there?"

What a great sense of humor she had and always ready to poke a little fun at herself.

Be the reason someone smiles today.
—Unknown

Rehearse Hard, Play Effortless

Many tennis players thrive during competition but can't bring that same joy and intensity to their practice. They rationalize this with several excuses, but the one that grates on me is, "I'd go for that ball in a *real* match." My thought is when running for *any* ball, if you get to it or not, you can learn something—whether it's adjusting a racket face or simply developing quickness on the court.

I once was watching Johnny Carson on *The Tonight Show* interview Bob Hope. We all remember the beautiful performances of Bob Hope and how effortlessly he performed his act. Johnny Carson made the statement, but Bob Hope's response resonated. Johnny said, "Bob, you make performing look so effortless." And Bob Hope responded, "It's because I rehearse so hard."

To my tennis enthusiasts: we only see the top players perform their tennis grace on the court during matches; it is so effortless. We aren't privy to the many difficult hours they rehearse (practice) their skills. There is no secret to improving—work harder with guidance from your tennis instructor *all the time.*

There is no glory in practice, but without practice there is no glory.

—Unknown

Another Bob Hope Story

Bob Hope was asked another question by Johnny Carson that night on the show. Carson's said, "I guess you've done this for so long, you no longer get nervous before you come on stage."

Bob Hope's reply was informative: "I still do get nervous every time I go on stage, but I choose to use it to motivate me to perform well."

It's not a bad thing to be nervous. It means you care.
—Dr. Jim Loehr

Fear of Winning?

I was privileged to work with a pro player, who made it to the Wimbledon semifinals in 1979, eventually losing to Roscoe Tanner. When I saw the player afterward, I asked him, "How did it feel walking onto the center court for the semifinals?"

His answer was illuminating: "I had a total feel of failure but also a total fear of success."

I said, "I understand the fear of failure but not the fear of success." Billie Jean King, however, understood. She famously said, *"A champion is afraid of losing. Everyone else is afraid of winning."*

The pro player went on to explain, and I paraphrase, that players invariably become familiar with losing and are taught how to handle losing gracefully; you know what is behind that "door." But players generally aren't coached in all the attendant results of winning a tournament that was a childhood dream: offers of endorsement, media frenzy, demands on their time, and playing in the finals of the championships.

Winning brings a different set of issues that can't be anticipated.
—Curly Davis

A Good Diet vs. A Bad Diet

A good diet has never won me a match, but a bad diet has lost me a match.

—Jim Courier, said to the author

I repeat this quote every time I hear a client lamenting a match lost because of "heaviness of legs" or "sluggishness" on the court.

I suggest that, when possible, they eat two hours ahead of the match to allow the digestive system to do its work. The following story illustrates the importance of diet.

I coached a German pro tour player, who was ranked #1,055 globally. He couldn't explain why he often experienced "heavy legs" during matches. I addressed his eating habits on our way to a pro tournament in Ft. Lauderdale. I offered the "good diet" adage and explained that his diet made him feel drained. He countered that he always ate steak and other heavy foods on match days because it made him feel strong. I insisted that eating correctly and hydrating the day before and the day of a match is the best way to peak performance.

Then we stopped at a market to buy sports drinks for the match. While going up and down the aisles, we passed the bakery where he saw some donuts, particularly "donut holes." He had never seen donut holes and asked, "What are these?" I explained what they were and how good they were.

Of course, he wanted to buy them, but I said, "NO! Not before your match; maybe once the tournament is over." I left him, found the sports drinks, and got three large bottles. I went to the checkout lane where he showed up carrying the box of a dozen donut holes with only six left in the box, proclaiming, "These are good," as he popped a seventh in his mouth. I said, "I told you, not now!"

We went onto the tournament; his match was played and was

over in less than an hour, losing 6–0, 6–1. He came off the court, complaining about feeling "bloated." My response was as expected: "And that's why I told you not to eat the donut holes!"

My message to him and all tennis players is that you train too hard and devote too much time and energy not to take care of things you *can* control. You can manage your equipment, attitude, effort, and diet.

"You can't out-exercise a bad diet."
—Unknown

Don't Interrupt Your Opponent When He Is Making Mistakes

During a tennis match, the opponent might go into a "walk-about," just walking around and not thinking about the match. When you observe this "walk-about" in your adversary, win as many points as you can without saying or doing anything to "wake up" the opponent. One such situation happened to me:

At the end of a long day of teaching tennis, I was in a tournament. I was in my thirties at the time, and playing against an eighteen-year-old, I was lethargic and uninterested in the match.

I found myself in a walk-about, which resulted in my being down in the first set 4–1. My young opponent ran after everything; he made good shots and felt good about his chances, but then *it* happened. He had an easy put-away at the net but hit it wide of his target. The ball landed out. He slammed his racket on the net and loudly said, "This is a joke. I'm having trouble beating an old man." I thought to myself, *Who's he calling an old man?!* I woke up from my walk-about and won the first set 6–4, then the second set 6–1.

We all find ourselves in that setting at some time. As we were shaking hands at the end of the match, I thought it best to give my opponent a lesson by saying, "Don't interrupt your opponent when they are sleeping." He looked at me with a "What does that mean?" look on his face.

Don't poke the sleeping bear.

—Unknown

The Other Shoe Just Dropped

One year at the National Boys' fourteen-and-under indoor championships in Chicago, I was coaching Michael. Michael loved to compete; all my practice sessions with him included competition. If not, he'd get bored. Michael's defining characteristic was his competitiveness; his will to win overcame any possible weakness in his game. His will made him the poster child for the axiom, "Will beats skill."

He was playing the match, lost the first set, and fought hard in the second set. He had a set point, but the opponent dug in and ran him from sideline to sideline. As Michael ran after the ball in full sprint, his left shoe came off, but that didn't stop him; he kept on running. He ran the ball down with one shoe off, hitting an outright winner up the line. He won the second set with that miraculous shot.

He came off the court with one shoe on and holding the other shoe in his hand. When I met him to discuss the match and what to do going forward, he interrupted me and said, "My shoe is too slow for me." I looked at him and thought, *He's joking around*. But knowing him as I did, he wasn't. My only logical response was, "Then let's go to the pro shop and buy you a pair of quicker shoes!

> *Winning isn't everything, but the will to win is everything.*
> —Vince Lombardi

Fight or Flight Signs

I pride myself on being able to read my students' body language and to understand what they are telling me without a word being said. I recognize whether they have understood a new teaching point, or if they are comfortable with attempting something new, or if they are in a fighting mode or a surrendering mode. These are all critical things that good tennis instructors/coaches intuit quickly.

As an example, I coached Laurie Stettler, a nationally ranked junior in the girls' eighteen-and-under and a senior in high school. Her talents were highly respected; she was sought after and was offered several scholarships to universities. She chose Notre Dame.

Laurie was highly seeded in a tournament in Lexington, Kentucky. The Notre Dame coach came to watch her play, as well as some other prospects. Laurie was in a hard-fought match that she could and should have won, but she was not showing me her "fight sign."

The Notre Dame coach stood beside me, two courts away, and asked, "What's going on with Laurie?" I had no answer for him at that moment, but then something happened. Laurie had dropped the first set and the second set was in contention when she came up to hit a short forehand and dumped it in the net. At that point, she picked the ball up and returned it to the other side; she then turned, threw the racket over her right shoulder, and slapped her left arm against her left leg so loud we could hear it from two courts away. She stormed back to the baseline with a determined stride.

I looked at the Notre Dame coach and said, "Okay, let's go watch other matches."

Surprised, he looked back at me and said, "But what about Laurie's match?"

"Oh, she'll win now because the *bitch* just showed up!" He asked me to explain, and I told him of Laurie's "fight sign." Her fight sign is throwing the racket on her right shoulder and slamming her hand against her leg. Laurie did go on to win the match.

Laurie didn't even know she did that. Laurie went to Notre Dame in the fall and came back to town during Christmas break and told me this story.

She played singles in a team match and was losing. When the coach came and sat by her court, Laurie missed a ball, and her fight sign came out. The coach got up and left. After the match, Laurie went up to the coach and asked, "Where'd you go?"

According to Laurie, his response was, "Curly told me about your fight sign, and you showed it. I knew then you would win the match."

She asked the coach what those fight signals were, and he responded by saying, "Ask Curly the next time you see him."

I informed her of her fight signs.

> *"F.E.A.R. has two meanings: 'Forget Everything And Run' or 'Face Everything And Rise.' The choice is yours"*
> —Zig Ziglar

Family Man

I attended the US Open men's finals in 1991 as both a tennis enthusiast and a TV reporter for WAVE-TV in Louisville, Kentucky. The contestants were Stefan Edberg and Jim Courier. As a TV reporter, I had access to many areas, including the players' lounge, where they would wait with their coaches, family, and/or entourage before being called onto the court.

The men's finals were scheduled to start, but because it was the opening day of professional football, the finalists had to wait for the "game of the day" to finish. All the televisions in the lounge were tuned to the station that would show the finals, so we all knew when the game of the day was over.

I saw Stefan Edberg sitting with his family, wife, and daughter on a couch in the players' lounge.

The tennis world would be viewing the match—several million viewers worldwide would see the match—but what I saw was something special. Stefan sat on the couch with his wife to his left and his infant daughter sitting on his lap, sucking on her father's finger as young infants do.

Watching this, I was impressed by his calmness before the match and, more importantly, the family unit around him. I thought, *This guy gets it.*

After the crowds stop applauding and the hero-worshipping ceases, we are all left with ourselves and our families.

> *Go through life wondering what is it all about but at the end of the day, it's all about family.*
>
> —Rod Stewart

(By the way, Stefan Edberg went on to win in straight sets, in one of the most beautiful serve-and-volley matches I have ever seen.)

6-0 ... A Scary Score

When you anticipate a challenging match against a good player, you go onto court ready! But what happens when you don't get the challenge you expect in the first set?

One such story: I was coaching a player in the girl's national eighteen-and-under in San Jose, California. The draw was tough; the girls were familiar with each other and knew it would be a tough, hard-fought match. But the first set was over in thirty minutes, with my player winning 6–0!

After the first set, I said to the mother of my player, "I don't like it. The score is too one-sided. There could be a letdown." And there was! My player let down just enough, and the opponent played a bit better, and the match turned.

When playing against an adversary and you expect a tough match,—but for whatever reason, you don't receive it—just play hard, not letting down. Momentum happens in tennis, just like in all sports.

> *What is imperative is to keep the momentum going. The difference between success and failure is very thin. The urge to win must be like a hunger inside you.*
>
> —Avijeet Das

Buy a Ticket!

My doubles partner and good friend, Sonny Garner, and I are both teaching pros and members of the United States Professional Tennis Association (USPTA). A tennis tournament is held each year at the USPTA national convention. The year I'm telling this story, the national convention was held in Chicago.

We played and won the tournament that year. With that win, we were ranked fifth among teaching pros. After winning the USPTA doubles tournament and being an optimist, I thought and spoke to Sonny about trying to get into the US Open the following year to play. He said, "Great! Let's see what happens."

I sent the United States Tennis Association (USTA) my inquiry about participating in the US Open doubles. I sent Sonny's and my playing résumé along with the investigation to the USTA.

A few weeks went by, and I received a letter from the USTA in response to my letter, which stated, "Your ticket inquiry is enclosed," and then read, "The only way you can get into the US Open is to buy a ticket!"

> *Defeat is not the worst of failures. Not to have tried is the true failure.*
>
> —George E. Woodberry

Facing Adversity

On another occasion, Sonny and I played in the Kentucky State indoor championships, and our match was very close. At a point in the match, Sonny hit a ball close to the baseline, and the opponents called it out. Sonny questioned the call rather aggressively.

When the opponents stayed with their call, Sonny looked at me and said, "Let's just tank (lose on purpose). I hit the perfect shot, and they called it out!" My response to Sonny was, "That's right ... we'll show them, we'll lose," in a sarcastic tone. I recommend to all athletes that when you get a dubious call, don't get mad; get more determined, and fight harder!

Winners never quit and quitters never win.
—Vince Lombardi

GALLERY

Don Kaiser and me

A View From Across the Net

Chapter Two

Adages I Use In My Teaching

"Learning happens when a conscious thought moves to an unconscious thought through repetition."
—Curly Davis

Students often want teaching pros to evaluate their game—what strokes to add or improve to make them more effective. We ask the student to think of each sequential movement the body needs to make to accomplish the goal. Invariably, after a few errors, the student will say, "I cannot think *and* play this game!"

My answer is, "How do *I* change something if *you* do not think?! My racket is not a magic wand where I can just wave it over you!"

A student of the game *must* think about the corrections they are being asked to perform; how else can one incorporate the new movements required? You must think, and then once you get a "feel" for the correction or new stroke, you must repeat it over and over. Repetition is the only way to move a conscious thought to unconscious thought.

"Do it until you get right, then do it some more until you can't get it wrong."
—Unknown

Excellent Tennis vs. Tennis Excellence

There is an old movie, *The Hustler*, with Jackie Gleason as Minnesota Fats, a billiards legend, and Paul Newman as Fast Eddie, a young, up-and-coming billiards player. The basic story is that Minnesota Fats becomes the mentor of Fast Eddie after watching him shoot pool for the first time and makes this observation: "Fast Eddie, you play excellent pool, but you don't have pool excellence."

We can apply this great statement to tennis: tennis IQ (tennis excellence) vs. tennis ability (excellent tennis). If two players are equal in ability, then tennis IQ will always win the match.

We have all had matches where we *knew* we were the better player: we were more technically sound with our strokes, better court movement, and a better tennis outfit! But the opponent won! WHY? Because they had *tennis excellence* while you may have had *excellent tennis*.

To me, *excellent tennis* means that you play a good game, have good strokes, and good execution. But *tennis excellence* is knowing where to hit the ball and where it will likely come back based on your shot placement. It is the mental battle we have during a match—with ourselves and the adversary, including overcoming outside influences like noise or weather. In short, tennis IQ, not just tennis ability.

Notice my definition of tennis IQ means being a *student* of the game, not just a participant in the game of tennis. Being a student of the game means you watch and observe tennis on TV and listen to the occasional wisdom of the commentators. Maybe you read tennis books, perhaps picking up more understanding from the author. Both will give you an insight into the thinking of a tennis player and their patterns and how to apply them to your game.

I am astonished when I ask a player, "What would you do if

you start losing a match? How would you turn it around?" Often the answer is, "I'll play better." Well, heck, if it was that simple, why didn't you do that when you came out on the court?

The answer for me is to *be a disruptor*. Disrupt your opponent. If you can't play better, bring their level down to your level. How do you do that? By using your tennis IQ—be smart. (You may have read my previous book, *Tennis . . . Play Smarter Not Harder*.) That is what I meant by "be smart." You can be innovative by changing your shots' speed or trajectory (higher or lower), playing farther back from the baseline or closer to the baseline, or using different spins. In short, be a disruptor and have tennis IQ.

"Will always beat skill, until skill unites with hard work."
—Curly Davis

Tennis Is a Game We Play Standing Sideways . . . Not Facing Toward the Front

Think about it! All stick sports (sports that have a hitting stick, e.g., baseball, golf, hockey, cricket, tennis) are played by turning our shoulders to the side of the oncoming ball to prepare for a "coiling" and "uncoiling" into the contact of the ball. Now, we do face forward when waiting for the ball to be struck, but we immediately turn and face sideways as soon as it is hit.

Big Points Don't Mean You Hit Big Shots

In every close match, there always is a "big point." The match could hinge on the outcome of this point. Often, especially in club doubles, a significant moment arrives and invariably the returner will take a big swing and try to direct it down the alley of the net opponent. Sometimes it may end up a winner, but it is a losing shot more often than not. *You do not need to go with a big shot.*

Take a lesson from the touring professionals. When one of the big points happens, watch and learn: They hit their most reliable shots to the biggest area of the court. An example is when you have a "breakpoint" and a second serve coming from the opponent; a big point opportunity presents itself.

When the server's ball toss goes up, you should step around to make sure you hit the most reliable, most confident stroke you have to the biggest court. This ensures that you are the first strike player and makes your foe react to your shot; you are in control. You are not hitting "out of control" or trying to hit a winner, but instead hitting a dependable but aggressive stroke. The more often you win the big points, the better chance you have of winning the match.

> *Big points do not mean you hit big shots; it means you hit the largest part of the court with your most reliable stroke.*
> —Unknown

Great Shots Win Points ... Good Shots Win Matches

Far too often, players are looking to hit a great shot when a good shot will suffice. An example of this is that person at your club who has a hard first serve, and when/if it goes in, they usually win the point, but I emphasize, *if* it goes in. My advice is to hit a good and reliable serve with 75 percent of their power.

Another example is hitting the down-the-line shot with many risks and minimal reward. I recommend hitting smart and good shots.

> *Play a game of percentages, not a game of perfection.*
> —Unknown

Tennis Players Are a Bunch of Losers!

Nine out of ten points are lost, not won, at the recreational level. Observe at your club that a mistake usually happens in the first four strokes; a serve, a return, and two groundstrokes, and the point is usually over.

My advice, be the winner by allowing your foe to be the loser.

Tennis Is a Very Negative Sport

The rules state that we are to tell our opponent if the ball did not land in the court by saying or indicating with an index finger: out, wide, long, fault, double fault. It does not state that we are supposed to tell them if their shot was "good." By hitting the ball back with no word or signal, we are giving the affirmative the ball was good. We also see that the commentators evaluate performances by counting unforced errors on TV. Additionally, tennis tournaments are negative; there may be 128 entries at the start of the tournament, and there will be 127 losers. There will be only one winner. Again, extremely negative.

The takeaway is that we play a negative sport, and when we start getting negative on ourselves or our partner, that weighs heavy on both, and it is hard to perform underneath that negativity. So, be your own cheerleader/supporter and stay positive.

> *"The entire sea of water can't sink a ship unless it gets inside the ship. Similarly, the negativity of the world can't put you down unless you allow it to get inside you."*
>
> —Goi Nasu

Why We Try to Hit Winners

A unique thought: all ball sports played with an object, ball, or puck have trained us to think that if we have the object, we are on offense; therefore, the opponent is on defense. And if we are on offense, we are trying to score a touchdown, basket, or goal.

Tennis is unique because we may have the ball on our side, but it does not mean we are on offense or defense. It depends on many situations—where you are on the court when you are hitting, where they are when they are hitting, having to hit your least preferred stroke, etc. Many situations require your proper response. But since we are trained to score, throw, sink, strike, shoot, we try to hit winners from anywhere on the court. Thus, it's one of the reasons why we try to hit winners at inopportune moments.

Just a thought.

You Don't Have to Be Perfect ... Just Better than the Person on the Other Side of the Net.

At his induction into the International Tennis Hall of Fame, Andre Agassi made that statement. He said, "I started to enjoy the game when I realized I did not have to be perfect, just better than the guy on the other side of the net."[1] It is a characteristic I have seen in many tennis players—they are perfectionists, including me!

Often, my clients tell me, "You are very patient," and I reply, "I am patient with you, but I would not be so patient with me if I make a mistake." But being a perfectionist is a double-edged sword; it is what drives you to be good, and it is what drives you nuts! When teaching someone, I never try to "kill" perfectionism; I try to manage it to be used in a good way.

Tennis is striving for perfection but never achieving it.
—Curly Davis

---

[1] From Andre Agassi's acceptance speech into the Hall of Fame.

"Success Breeds Complacency."
—Andy Grove

Sometimes success, or winning, breeds a complacent attitude and actions, as this story illustrates:

Immediately after a boxer had just won a fight, the press was interviewing his trainer and asked, "What do you need to work on with your fighter?"

With his boxer standing next to him, the trainer answered, "He needs to work on his right cross and keep his hands up when he throws a punch."

The fighter heard this and said to his trainer, "Yeah, but I won!"

The trainer turned toward his student and said, "So do you have to *lose* before you listen?"

When athletes win, they can fall into the trap of believing it is due to their natural ability. They may forget the hard work that got them there and the ongoing hard work that is needed to maintain their level.

> *Beware of success. It can knock you into a fixed mindset: "I won because I have talent. Therefore, I will keep winning." Success can infect a team or it can infect an individual.*
> —Carol S. Dweck, *Mindset: The New Psychology of Success*

"Sometimes It's What Your Opponent Did Right, Not What You Did Wrong."
—BBC TV Commentator

A player will often lose a point during a lesson and ask, "What did I do wrong?" Most of the time, they are correct in asking that question, but now and then, an opponent will just hit a good shot. Then my answer is, "The opponent hit a good shot. Applaud and say, 'nice shot.' You did nothing wrong."

"Progress Today Determines Tomorrow's Achievements."
—Unknown

I love this quote. I do not know who said it, and I am sure it was not intended for tennis, but it is very apropos. I often use it when I see my students get frustrated not performing the stroke they are being taught. It encourages the students to trust in the process of working on strokes and gives faith that today's work will pay off in the future. I stress to my students that learning doesn't travel in a straight line; there are lots of ups and downs.

A story to illustrate: I was teaching Greta Gibson, from Little Rock Arkansas, a highly ranked junior with an excellent two-handed backhand, and I wanted her to add a one-handed backhand slice to her game. Knowing that she would fight any change if it didn't happen instantly, I had to convince her that the process leads to the product.

I came on the court with a sign taped to the front of my teaching cart that read: "Progress Today Determines Tomorrow's Achievements." She was trusting as I explained why we were adding the one-handed backhand slice, then explained the biomechanics of the one-handed slice backhand, and finally, explained the plan for incorporating it in her game.

But later, as mistakes started to add up, she was frustrated and started asking, "Why are we doing this?" Every time she questioned it, I did not argue with her; I just pointed to the sign on the front of my teaching cart. I am happy to say that she owned the one-handed backhand slice within one week, and it served her well. She won the Southern Girl's eighteen-and-under and went to Baylor with a tennis scholarship.

Above, I use the terms "trust" and "why." I have found that when being coached by a teaching pro, you will learn quickest by trusting what they are adding to your game. Now that doesn't mean you should not ask "why." This "why" can come in two varieties: The first is an argumentative "why"—"Why do I have to do this?" This is certainly a waste of time. The alternative is an understanding "why"—"Why does this help my game?" This "why" shows the coach's vision of how and when the new stroke can best be used to advantage.

Trust combined with faith equals accomplishment.
—Unknown

"Put Your Racket Out; Something Good May Happen." —Harry Hopman

The great Australian Davis Cup coach, plus coach to many touring pros, Harry Hopman would often tell his prodigies, "Put your racket out; something good may happen." Far too often, players will watch a ball go by them and do nothing, thinking they have no chance to reach the ball. Do as Harry would encourage his students to do: put your racket out, and maybe— just maybe—the ball will hit your frame or strings, and you will get lucky. We all have had that happen to us and for us! Plus, we know the ball will not detour from its flight and try to find your racket!

A related thought: After hitting a miss-hit winner, players often will joke, "I paid for the whole racket; I'll use the whole racket." Applying that same advice to the ball's placement: Why use only *one* target on the court? *You paid for the whole court; use the entire court!*

"You Don't Pay the Price of Success, You Enjoy the Benefits." —Zig Ziglar

I worked at the Louisville Tennis Club, an indoor/outdoor facility. One Sunday, I was indoors coaching a young tennis star, Liz Cecil. Liz was small in stature but big in heart, made you earn every point you won, she gave her opponent no "cheap" points. Liz was a hard worker during lessons, willing to work on aspects of her tennis game to improve, laser-focused, and very coachable. In short, she would listen and make every attempt to try what I was asking.

As a result of Liz's hard work, focus, and good wins at tournaments, she was ranked #3 in the nation, in the girls' eighteen-and-under. Being such a highly ranked player, she was often invited to represent the United States in team competitions against other countries. Liz had just gotten back to Louisville from one of those team competitions with an all-expenses-paid stay in San Francisco. But this day, she seemed distracted, almost uninterested in the lesson. I tried getting her attention by changing drills, then changing my approach by joking more but neither worked.

We came to a time in the lesson where we took a short break for water, towel off, etc. A girlfriend of Liz's came on the court said to Liz, "A group of us are going to the mall, you want to come?" Liz thought and said, "No, I have to go to fitness after this lesson."

After the break and conversation with her friend, I noticed Liz was even more disinterested in the lesson. I called her to the net and asked, "What's bothering you?"

She replied, "I would rather go to the mall with my friends than be here working on my tennis and fitness." She went on to say, "I guess I have to pay the price."

I quickly responded with, "You don't pay the price ... you

enjoy the benefits of your success." I reminded her of the benefits she enjoyed, the all-expenses-paid trip to San Francisco, her other trips, and traveling to cities. The commitment to being the best you can be at your chosen activity knowing distractions will arise, and you must stay committed to your goal.

Where there is a commitment, there will be a sacrifice.
—Unknown

"A Tennis Player Is Only as Good as Their Weakness." —Pancho Gonzales

I was honored, on many instances, to be selected as coach to Kentucky Davis Cup and Fed Cup junior team competitions. We competed against other southern state teams in both singles and doubles. On this occasion, we were in Little Rock, Arkansas, at Burns Park, a friendly park setting with fifteen tennis courts, many situated all in a row.

In this team match, Kentucky had four courts of boys playing singles simultaneously and in a row next to each other. A unique sidebar to this team competition, the coaches were allowed to talk/coach during the matches. I was roaming back and forth behind the fence, taking quick looks at each match. Where needed and observed, I would call my player over to offer my insights on strategy.

I walked behind one of the boy's courts and stopped to watch. One of my players had a "loser walk" about him, shoulders down, head down, no energy in his walk between points. Sensing he needed some encouragement, I called him over to the fence and told him, on the next point, "serve and volley."

He said back to me, "I did that, Coach, and it didn't work."

My response was, "Then stay back and moon ball him, get him out of his rhythm."

My player looked and me and said, "Coach . . . I did that too, and it didn't work."

Sensing his dilemma and his frustration, I told him, "Call your opponent to the net and fart on him! Maybe that will distract him!" We both laughed; he had a quicker step to him then. I was imparting to him that the opponent has a weakness, you must find it, exploit it, and for the rest of the match, everything you do is make them play their weakness.

I have never lost a match; I didn't find my opponent's weakness in time . . . on many occasions.
—Unknown

"Prepare and Wait . . . Don't Wait to Prepare." —Jimmy Evert

This statement was a saying from the father and coach of Chris Evert, Jimmy Evert, to get every student to understand the importance of preparation in our sport, but it would hold for all sports. Do not wait to prepare; get the racket ready, get over to where the ball will be early, then wait for the ball to arrive.

"Be Quick So You Don't Hurry." —John Wooden

In his terrific book, *They Call Me Coach*, the legendary UCLA basketball coach John Wooden would often say, and I echo the quote frequently, especially when a student is slow to prepare, "Be quick, so you don't hurry."

Tennis is an emergency sport—the ball is flying at you quickly, and you only have a short time to prepare. Many players delay preparing because they do not anticipate well or do not sense the emergency setting.

His advice and mine are: Be quick to the ball, be quick in your racket prep, and be quick in your shot selection. If you are quick in *these* components, you will slow down the game, so you will not hurry your swing. You speed up your preparation so you can slow down your thinking.

"We Are Very Good for the Time We Don't Practice." —Harry Hopman

Often, I am asked, "Do you see any improvement in my game?" I respond with the question, "How often do you go out and practice? And playing a match, although it may be fun, is not practicing."

Their response usually is "not often" or "I'm playing on so many teams that I don't have the time." For improvement in tennis, as in life, *"You get what you give."*

Recreational players warm up for five minutes and then say, "I'm not going to get any better; let's play!" That's usually the extent of practicing that people do. As the title reads, we are particularly good for only practicing for five minutes and then playing.

I recommend the following three times a week with a practice partner. (You are Player "A" and practice partner player "B.") These are cooperative drills, and no one is trying to win points:

- Ten minutes of hitting down-the-line (Player A deuce side, Player B in ad court).
- Ten minutes of hitting down-the-line (Player A in ad court, player B in deuce court).
- Ten minutes of hitting cross-court (Player A in ad court, Player B in deuce court).
- Ten minutes of hitting cross-court (Player A deuce court, Player B in ad court).
- Ten minutes of Player A at the net, Player B at baseline.
- Ten minutes of Player A at baseline, Player B at net.
- Ten minutes of Player A serving, Player B returning.

- Ten minutes of Player A returning, Player B serving.

Try this for one hour and twenty minutes three times a week, and I guarantee you will see much improvement.

Practice isn't the thing you do once you're good. It's the thing you do to make you good.
—Malcolm Gladwell

"There Are No Bad Feeds, Just Bad Footwork." —Harry Hopman

Scenario #1: The instructor feeds the ball to the student; the student makes a mistake on the fed ball. They will often say (perhaps jokingly), "BAD FEED!" My response is, there are no bad feeds, just bad footwork. Footwork puts you in an excellent position to make a technically sound swing every time.

Scenario #2: The instructor's feed lands out; the student will say, "Out." Again, if you get to an "out" ball, then an "in" ball ought to be easy to get. So, hustle to every ball, and when match time comes, you will find yourself constantly in the proper position and place to hit the ball.

Bad feeds may explain the bad results...but it doesn't excuse the poor footwork.

"Pressure Is a Privilege."
—Billie Jean King

It is a given that there will be pressure in any sport or business; often, whoever handles this pressure better is the winner.

To handle the pressure, we must first recognize it, and tennis has its distinctive burdens:

Scoreboard Pressure: Often, scoreboard pressure is a "swing point"—30–15 or 30–30—each of these points adds pressure because it could mean extending or losing the lead. **Game pressure** is at the 4–3 game (seventh game), which could tie the score if you win or grow your opponent's lead if you lose.

Court Pressure: When you or your opponent move inside the baseline or take the net position. This adds pressure for the person staying back to hit a small target area; if they don't, the net person will likely win the point.

Spin Pressure: The spin we apply to the ball can add pressure by bouncing higher (topspin) or lower (slice), moving the ball up or down out of the comfort zones. Also, sidespin (often seen with a drop-shot) adds pressure when the ball hits and spins sideways off the court.

Power Pressure: We all know about this. By hitting harder, the ball zips through the court much faster, giving the opponent very little time to prepare.

Placement Pressure: Hitting the ball close to the baseline doesn't allow the opponent time to return an offensive ball. Or by repeatedly hitting the ball to the weaker stroke, you might force an uncomfortable feeling or eventually a complete pressure breakdown.

Tennis: Intensity Without Tension

Coaches tell you to "play with intensity," but sometimes the result is that your muscles tense up, and you lose fluidity on your strokes. Then you try to relax and lose your intensity. To find the balance, you must play with passion—go for all your opponent's shots, but once you get to the ball, relax your muscles to allow the arm and legs to move freely. Play intense without being tense.

Intensity is the price of excellence.
—Warren Buffet

"If You Can Feel the Change, You Can Own the Change." —Unknown Golf Pro

When teaching tennis to students, coaches will suggest changes or add strokes to their game. Once the students get the "feel" of the newly acquired stroke, they can "own" the change by replicating the change repeatedly.

All progress is change, but not all change is progress.
—John Robert Wooden

Inconsistent Ball Toss, Inconsistent Serve

As we know, the serve is the most important stroke in tennis. One critical part of making it consistent or inconsistent is the ball toss. Not being able to predict where the ball will be on contact makes for a very uncertain and unconfident serve. Players quite often try to "rescue" a bad ball toss; the ball should "find" the swing, not the swing "finding" the ball. Try serving with your eyes closed—if you have a consistent ball toss, you will still contact the ball.

I've never seen a consistent serve with an inconsistent ball toss.

—Brad Gilbert

CAN'T WIN THE DERBY ON A DONKEY

I had the pleasure of coaching many highly ranked players throughout my career. I like to think I helped them achieve their dreams, but the players' talents with an assist "steering" always brought them success.

One such story: I was at the girls' sixteen-and-under Southern Tennis Championships in Atlanta, Georgia. I had started coaching Betsy just before the tournament. She had two qualities I liked: talent and thirst. Talent to execute the new strokes I was teaching and the thirst for learning more—a successful combination for any player. I was excited to see how she would perform with the new "tools" we had just added.

Betsy drew the number-two-seeded player in the tournament. I watched Betsy play an excellent match, and she won. After the match, the person's mother who lost to Betsy came to me and asked, "Are you Betsy's coach?"

Because I didn't know where she was going with this question, I answered cautiously, "Yes."

The mother responded, "Will you coach my daughter? I have seen Betsy play in the past, and I noticed a big difference in today's tennis game. I want a coach to help my daughter to keep improving, and she's not getting that. Can you coach her?"

Betsy won the match and, by doing so, made me a coach others wanted to be coached by. To begin with, she had the talent; all I did was "steer" her in the right direction. Second, we as coaches need to remind ourselves:

Players make coaches . . . Coaches don't make players.
—Unknown

Carrot or Kick

When coaching a player, you must know when the right time to criticize their effort is in order to get more out of them, more than they think they have—looking each day into their moods and tolerance for criticism. Note I said *criticize* their effort, because as a coach we must always let the student know it's a performance, not a personality we condemn. A rule the military has that may serve you well:

> *Compliment in public, criticize in private.*
> —Unknown

You Get What You Give

When you hit a tennis ball at a steep angle to send it "off the court," you assume you have just put your opponent in a world of hurt. But sometimes, they hit it back at an even better angle than yours! And you end up losing the point. How does this happen?

Your super angle gave your opponent a better angle back to you: they can hit the angle because you *gave* them the angle.

In short, we give an angle, and we get an angle.

This saying can also apply to life. I often tell my juniors who aren't applying themselves, "Why would you expect one-hundred-percent good results with only a fifty percent effort? What you give is what you can expect in return."

> *The amount of effort you put in is the amount of results you end up with.*
> —Unknown

Plan the Play ... Then Play the Plan

When playing a point in tennis, players often change their minds mid-swing, which invariably leads to a mistake. As a coach, I want my players to have clarity of thought. This clarity comes from having a plan and then staying with that plan.

A road map gives us a plan for arriving at the destination, but since there may be unknown hurdles and pitfalls along the way, it doesn't *guarantee* our arrival.

We can plan, but we can't predict.
—Unknown

IF NOTHING CHANGES ... THEN NOTHING CHANGES

Recently I was watching a professional women's tennis match on TV. One competitor was right-handed and the other left-handed. To set the picture for you, the right-handed participant had won the first set and was serving for the match at 5–2 in the second set.

The score was deuce, and the right-handed participant won the point, taking the score to her ad, match point for her. Her first serve was a fault; the second serve went in, but to the left-hander's forehand where she unleashed a great forehand down-the-line for an outright winner. It went back to deuce.

At deuce, the right-hander won the point, and again had match point. The first serve was a fault; the second serve went to the lefty's forehand and—*BAM!*—another forehand winner down-the-line. It went back to deuce.

Right-hander won the deuce point for a third match point! She got the first serve in! *But* it went to the left-hander's forehand and...? You guessed it: another winner down-the-line!

Right-hander won the deuce point, and it went to her ad, yet another match point—her fourth. By this time, I am screaming at the TV (as you would too), "Serve it to the backhand!" (Like she could hear me.) She did serve to her backhand, and after a long rally, the right-hander won the point and the match. Any of us watching on TV could have given her the answer, but it took three times for her to serve somewhere else.

Why, in a match, do we become just as stubborn as this right-handed player did? Thinking, *I'll serve it to the forehand again*, or *I'll get that ball down their alley eventually, but I'll keep trying until I make one.* Winning one point at the cost of losing five makes for a failing tactic.

> *I can't change the direction of the wind, but I can adjust my sails to always reach my destination.*
> —Jimmy Dean

"You May Have Sixteen Golf Clubs to Choose From, But You Only Have One Swing." —Jack Nicklaus

In tennis, it is the same. We may have several options to choose from when we're hitting the ball, but we should only have one swing technique. Multiple swings make for unpredictable results.

> *Success is simple. Do what's right, the right way, at the right time.*
> —Arnold H. Glasow

You Teach . . . You Touch

This is a saying I love, and it inspires me each day that I teach this wonderful game. It lets me realize that when I am on the court teaching people, I am touching their life through tennis and may have an impact on them.

One such story, I was once at a park in Louisville, Kentucky, known as Shawnee Park. I was approached by one of the mothers of a girl I taught. She asked if I had fifteen minutes to teach her the basics of serving after I was through with teaching the girls, and I said, "Sure."

The next day, when I finished teaching the young girls, I started teaching the mother who asked for a serving lesson. I taught her an extremely basic 1-2-3 serve approach: (1) the preparation—body weight evenly distributed, arms in front pointing toward the net; (2) both arms going up, left arm tossing the ball, right arm with the racket going up and falling behind her back; (3) the racket moving up to the ball and finishing to the left side of her body. We repeated that over and over—1-2-3, 1-2-3. When I left, she understood the serving motion. I did not see her again at the park.

About fifteen years later, I taught at an indoor club in Louisville. I was standing in the lobby where many people were coming to play or just finishing. A lady came up to me and asked, "Do you remember me?" I was honest and said, "Sorry, I don't." She responded by going into a serving motion and said, "One-two-three!" It was her! She said, "I never forgot that simple serving technique you taught me, and ever since, I have enjoyed playing the game of tennis because of that one lesson." We had an excellent time remembering that lesson in Shawnee Park.

The second story I share needs a bit of background. I was giving lessons to a young gentleman applying to colleges for admission. Instructions given by the colleges were to tell of someone who affected your life significantly, not part of your family. His father brought me his essay. The following is what he wrote:

> The fuzzy yellow balls fly at me like bullets, relentlessly moving me back and forth to return them to the other side of the net. My tennis coach, Curly Davis, stands by his basket, armed with more tennis balls to send my way. "Keep a wider stance when you turn on your backhand side," he shouts enthusiastically, taking a sip of his favorite soda. After hitting a few more good balls, Curly predictably calls me up to the net. I know what is coming, and I can barely keep a smile from cracking across my face. Each lesson, I look forward to the moment when Curly tells me some inspirational quote or joke about life. Today, he says, "Books give you knowledge, people give you wisdom."
>
> He amazes me because he not only knows so many inspirational sayings but he takes the time to pass them on to me in a way that no one ever has or will. Rather than simply reciting vacuous quotes, Curly inspires me by truly making them his own. As soon as I arrive, he asks me about the date of my next standardized test or debate tournament, always ready to share his wisdom with me through helpful suggestions and motivation. Although it is not Curly's job to impart such wisdom, he takes the time to do so because that is his natural character. If Curly simply did his job, like so many of us are guilty of doing, then I would not be the person I am today.
>
> Curly's quote is true—while I have read many books, they have only given me knowledge. I have yet to read a book that has inspired me to do so many things, as have Curly and his free-flowing wisdom. From the truly profound to the plainly

simple, I use the many elements of wisdom passed on from Curly daily to enhance my growing knowledge base so I can make confident, well-informed decisions in every sector of my life. Wherever life takes me and whomever it brings across my path, I will always consider Curly to be one of my most significant influences.

You never know what people will remember and how it will affect them. After writing both stories, I am grateful and realize I am successful because I have helped many.

www.ingramcontent.com/pod-product-compliance
Lightning Source LLC
Chambersburg PA
CBHW071902070526
44583CB00016B/1807